HORSES IN ART

A *COLORING* book

Angie McPherson

Copyright © 2018 by Angela McPherson

All rights reserved.

ISBN-13: 978-1725790681

ISBN-10: 1725790688

Works of Equine Art:

1. William K. Hewitt, "Washington Crossing the Delaware," 1838-1846.
2. Emi-Jean Horace Vernet, "An Algerian Lady Hawking," 1839.
3. Warne & Co., "Trolley Master," 1880.
4. Johann Elias Ridinger, "Horse," 17th & 18th century.
5. Circus Show bill, unknown origin, date
6. Albrecht Dürer, "The Large Horse," 1505.
7. Théodore Géricault, "Boy Feeding a Cart Horse from Nose Bag," 1822.
8. Célestin Nanteuil, "Horse Before the Race," 1813-1873.
9. Diego Velazquez, "Don Gasper De Guzman, 1635.
10. Anthony Van Dyck, "A Man Riding a Horse," 1630.
11. Ishikawa Toyonobu, "Young Samurai Riding on Horseback, 1711-1785.
12. François Clouet, "Henry II, King of France," 1536-1572.
13. Stefano della Bella, "A Horseman atop a Rearing Horse," 1642-1645.
14. Series from William S. Kimball & Co, "Pet Horse from Household Pet Series, 1891.
15. Peter Nicolai Arbo, "Dagr," 1874.
16. Eugene Delacroix, "Goetz van Belichingen's Horse," 1842.
17. Jacques-Louis David, "Napoleon Crossing the Alps," 1801.
18. Caravaggio, "Conversion on the Way to Damascas," 1601.
19. Odilon Redon, "The Captured Pegasus," 1889.
20. Charles Edouard Boutibonne, "Empress Eugenie," 1857.
21. Louis Icart, "Lady Wind with a Black Horse," 1880-1950
22. Frederick Remington, "The Cowboy," 1902.
23. William Blake, "The Horse," 1805.
24. Henri de Toulouse-Lautrec, "At the Circus: The Spanish Walk," 1899.
25. Ludwig Koch, "Lipizzaner with Rider," 1866-1934.

Public Domain works courtesy of The Met: https://www.metmuseum.org/art/collection

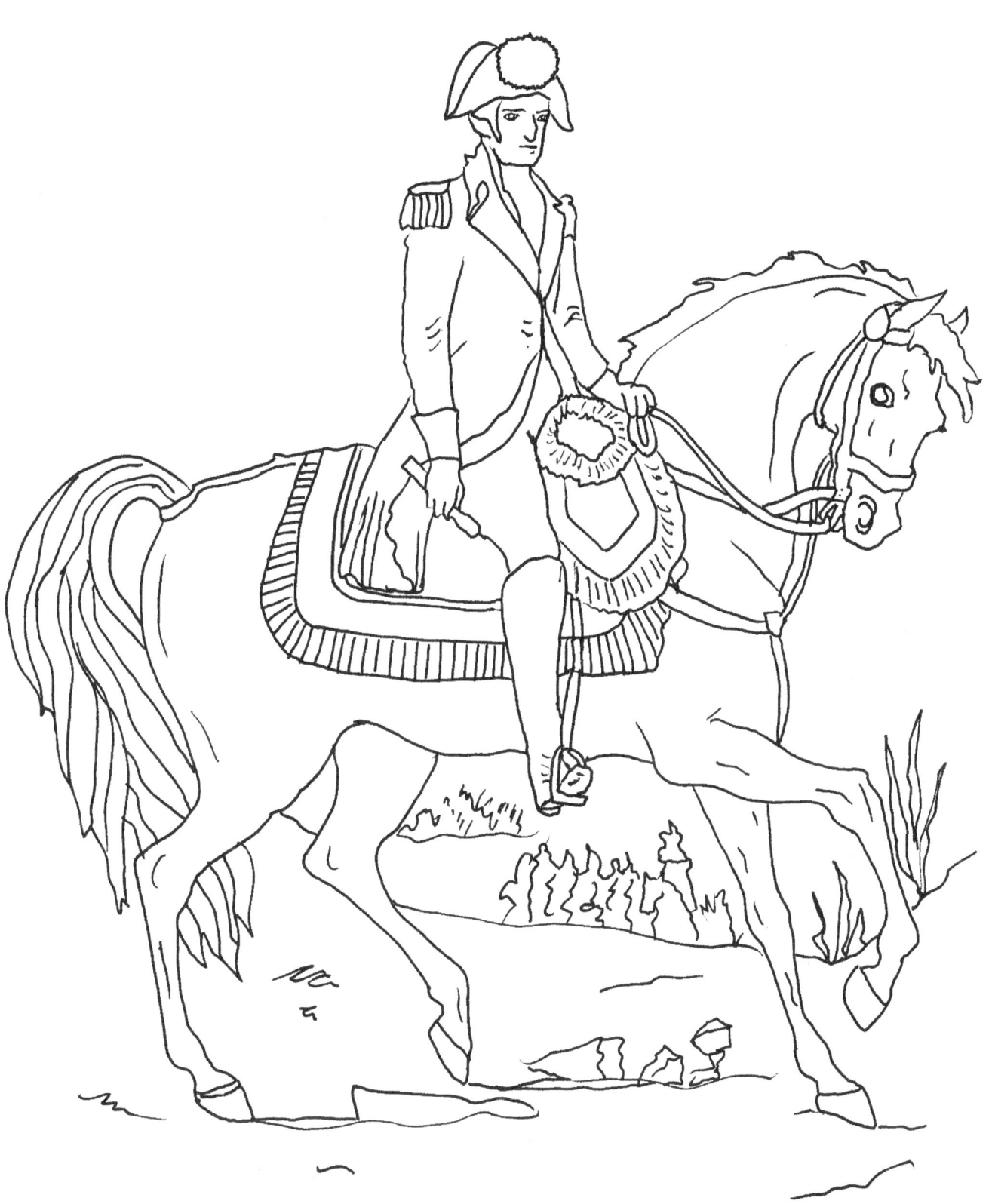

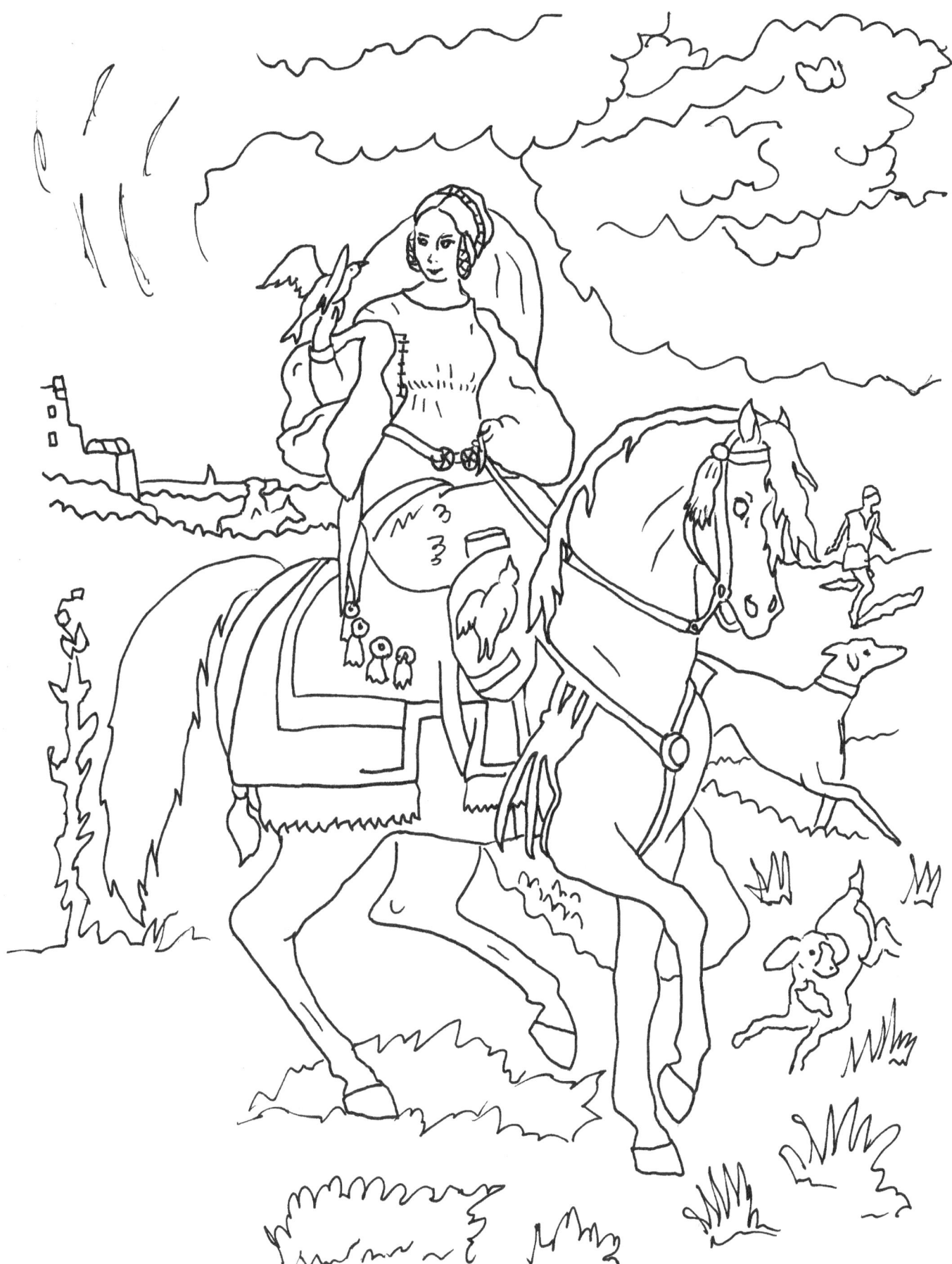

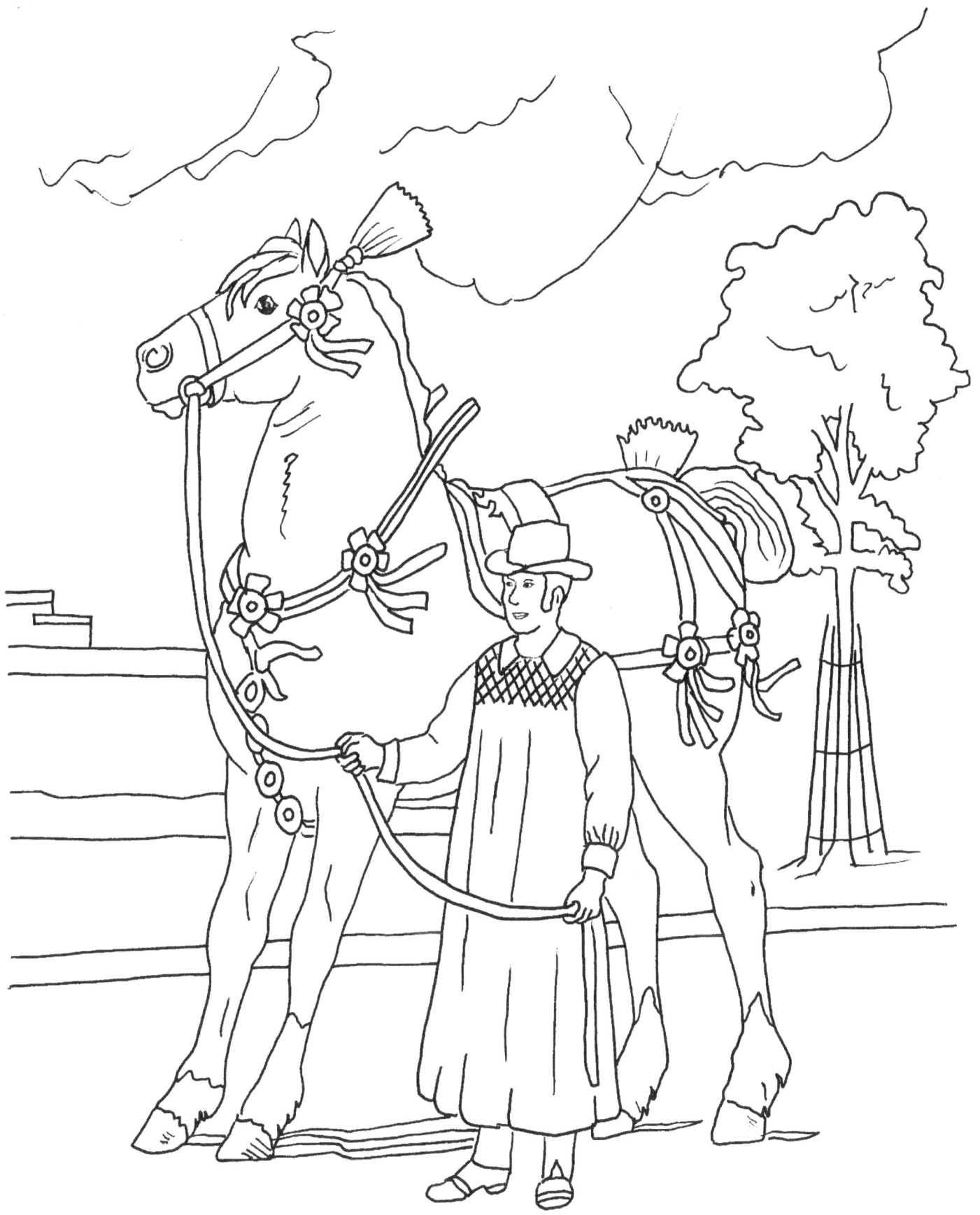

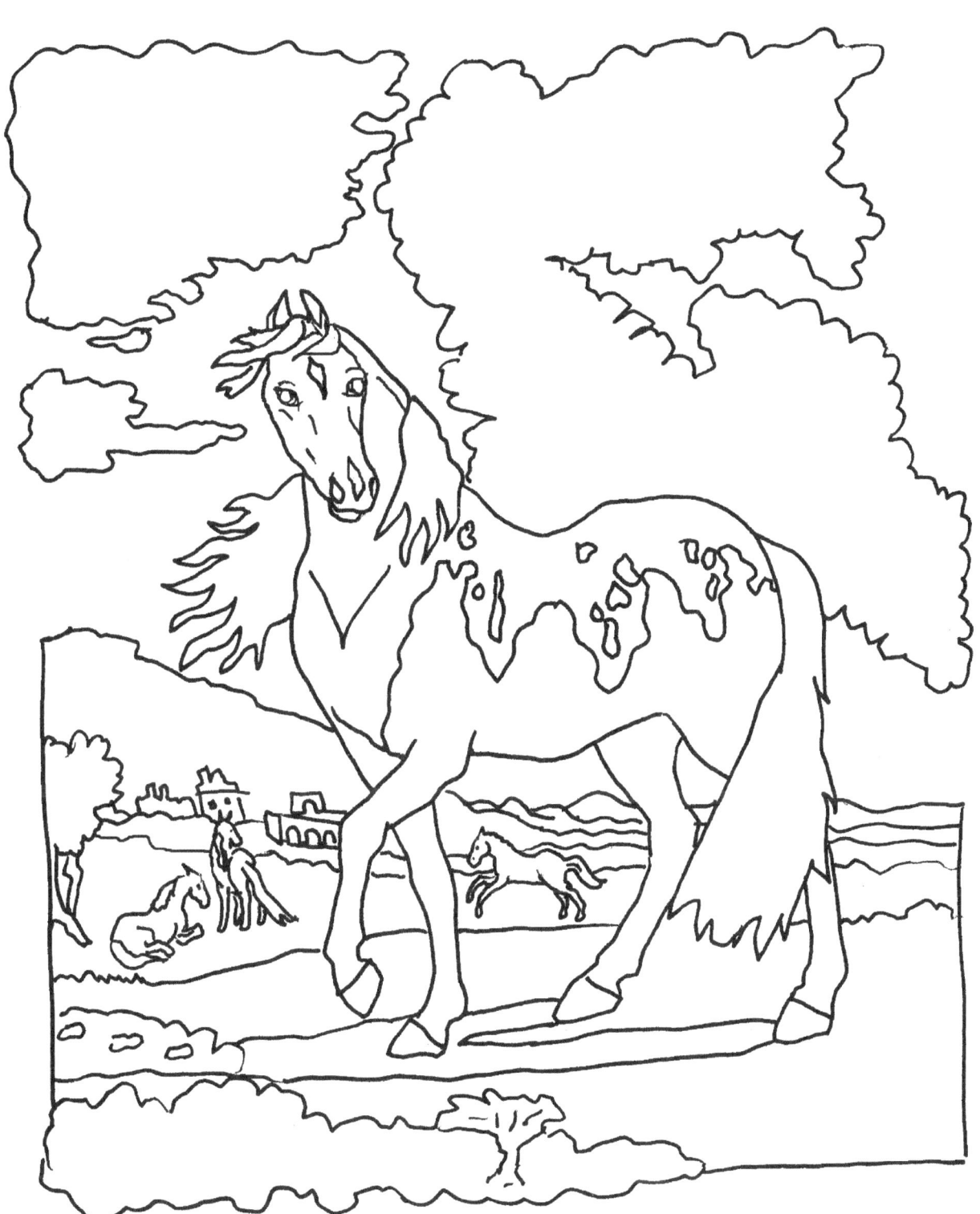

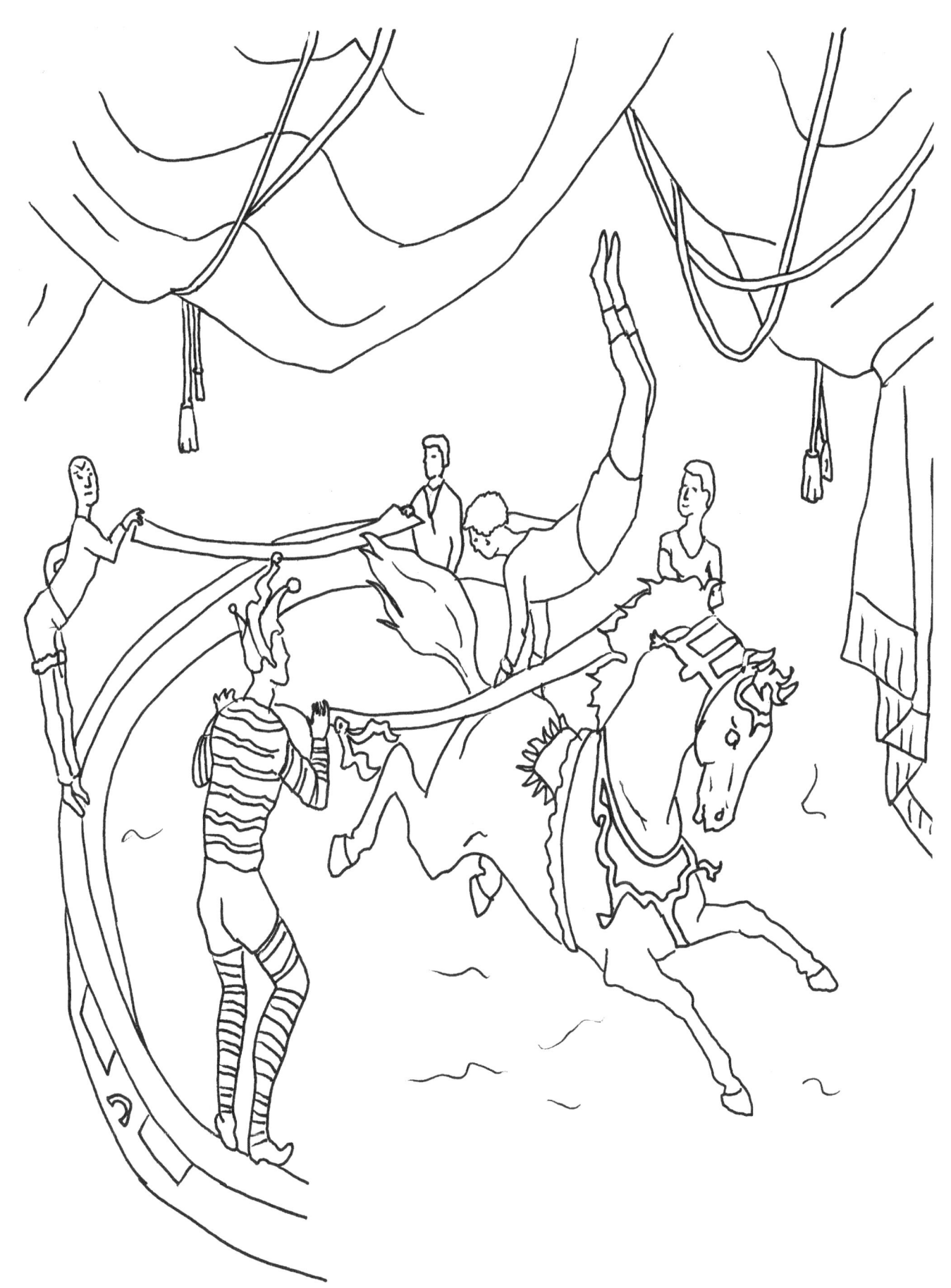

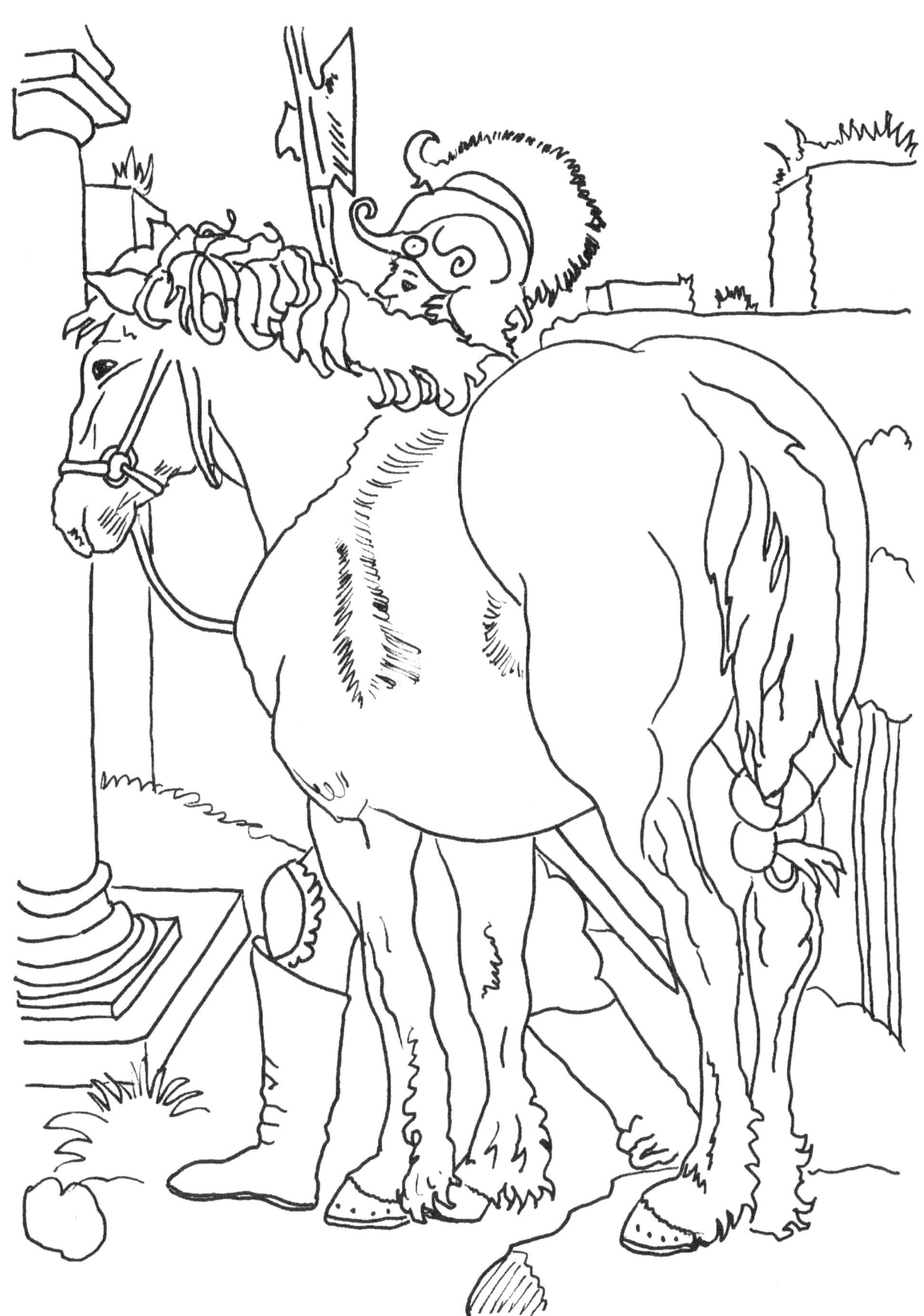

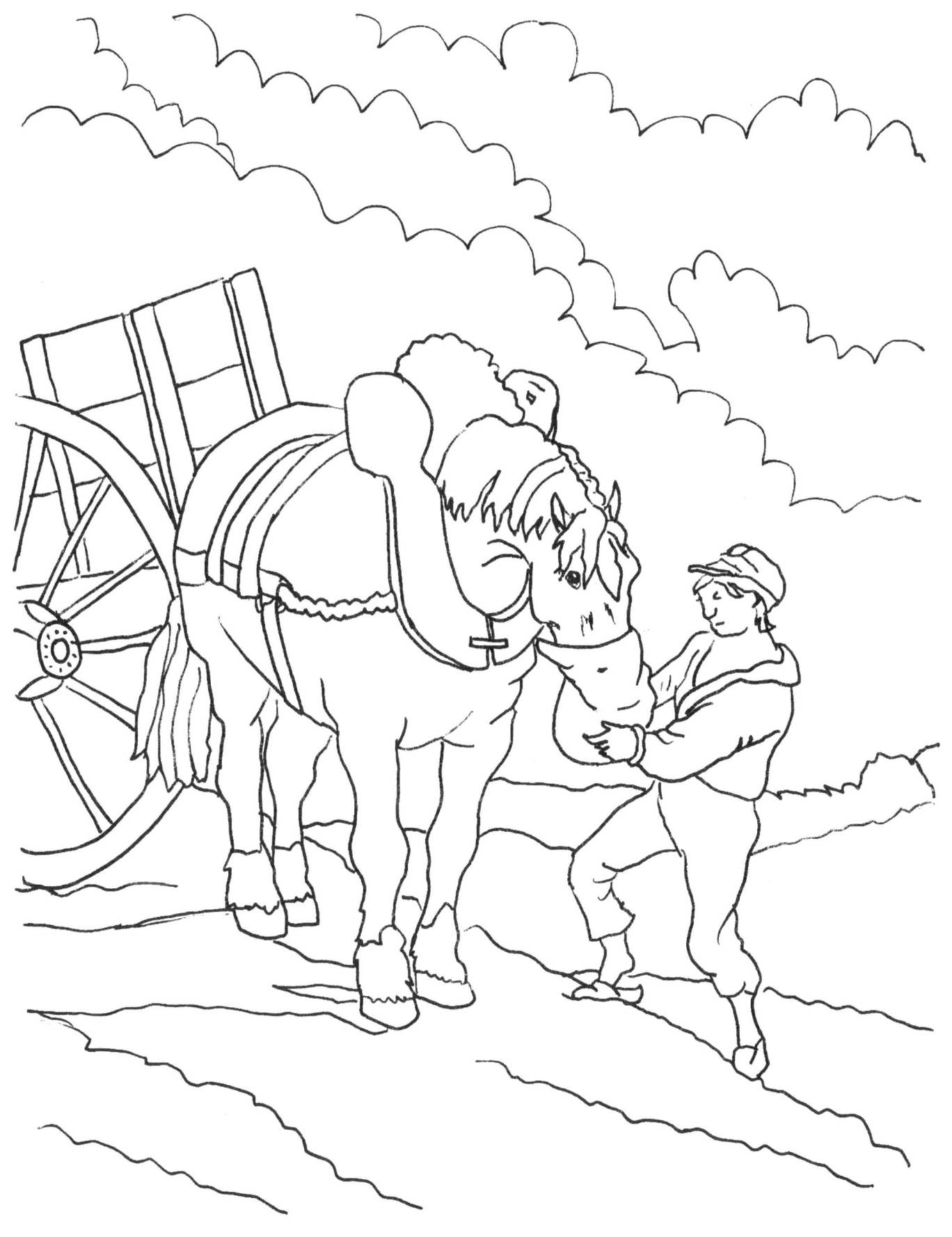

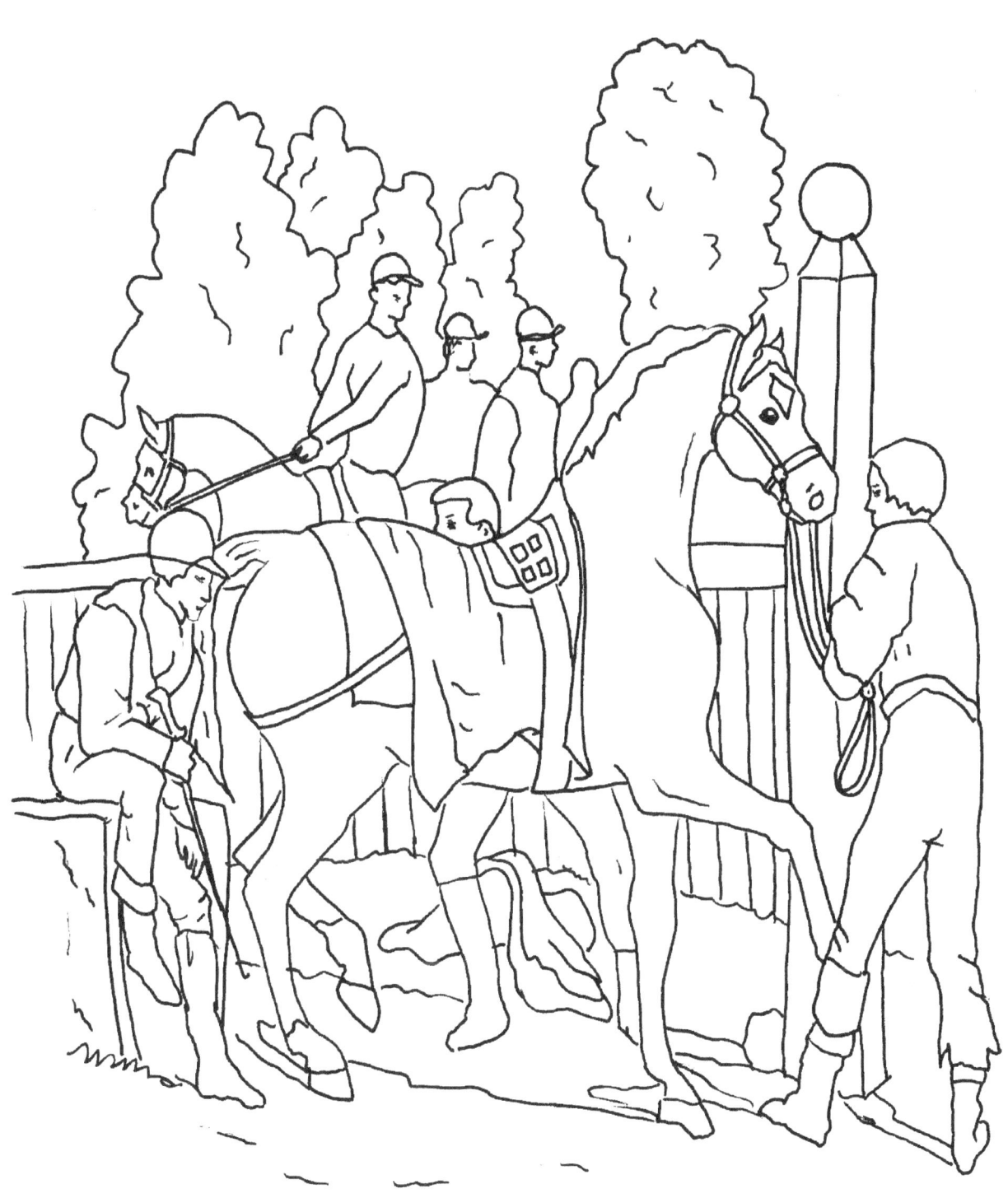

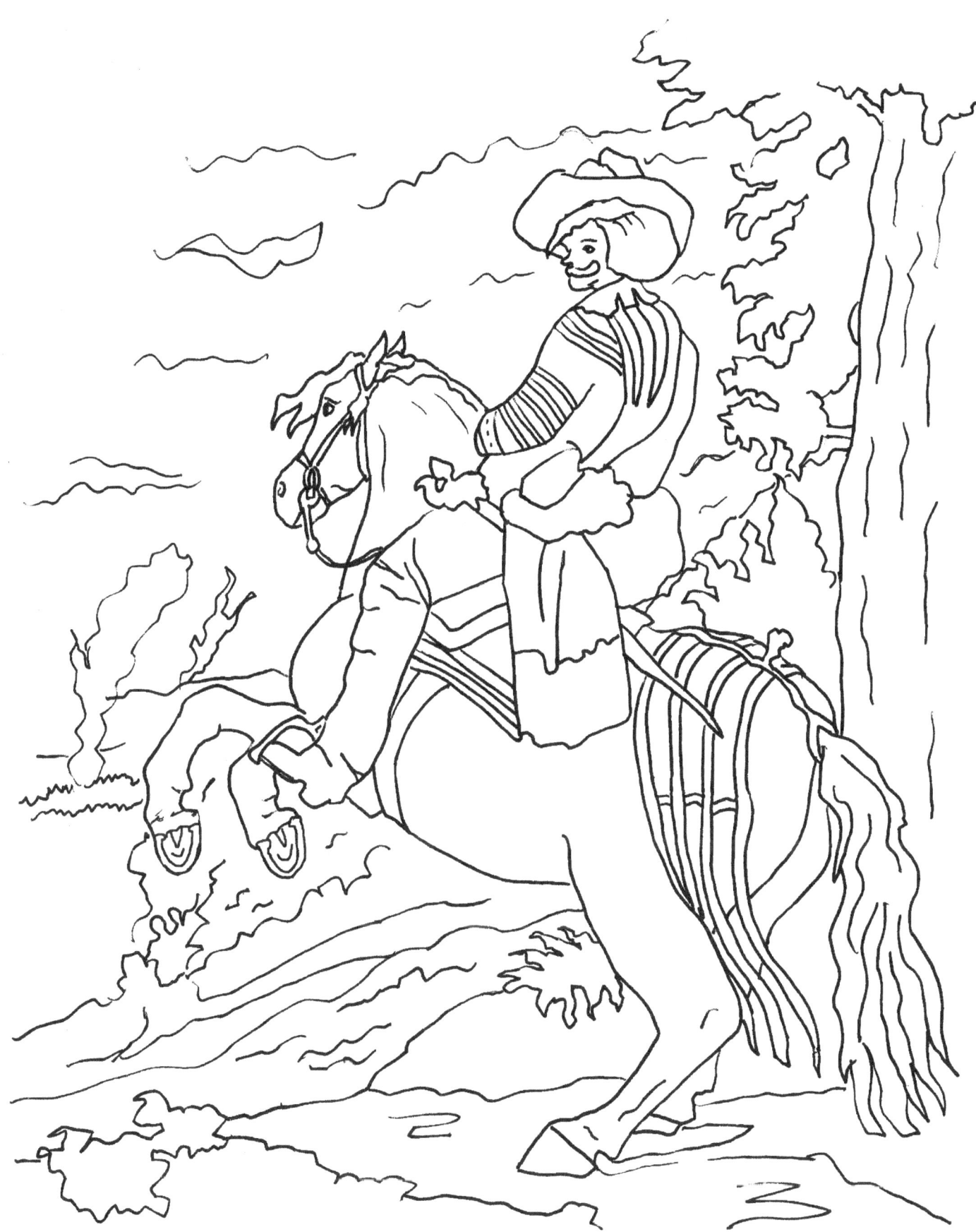

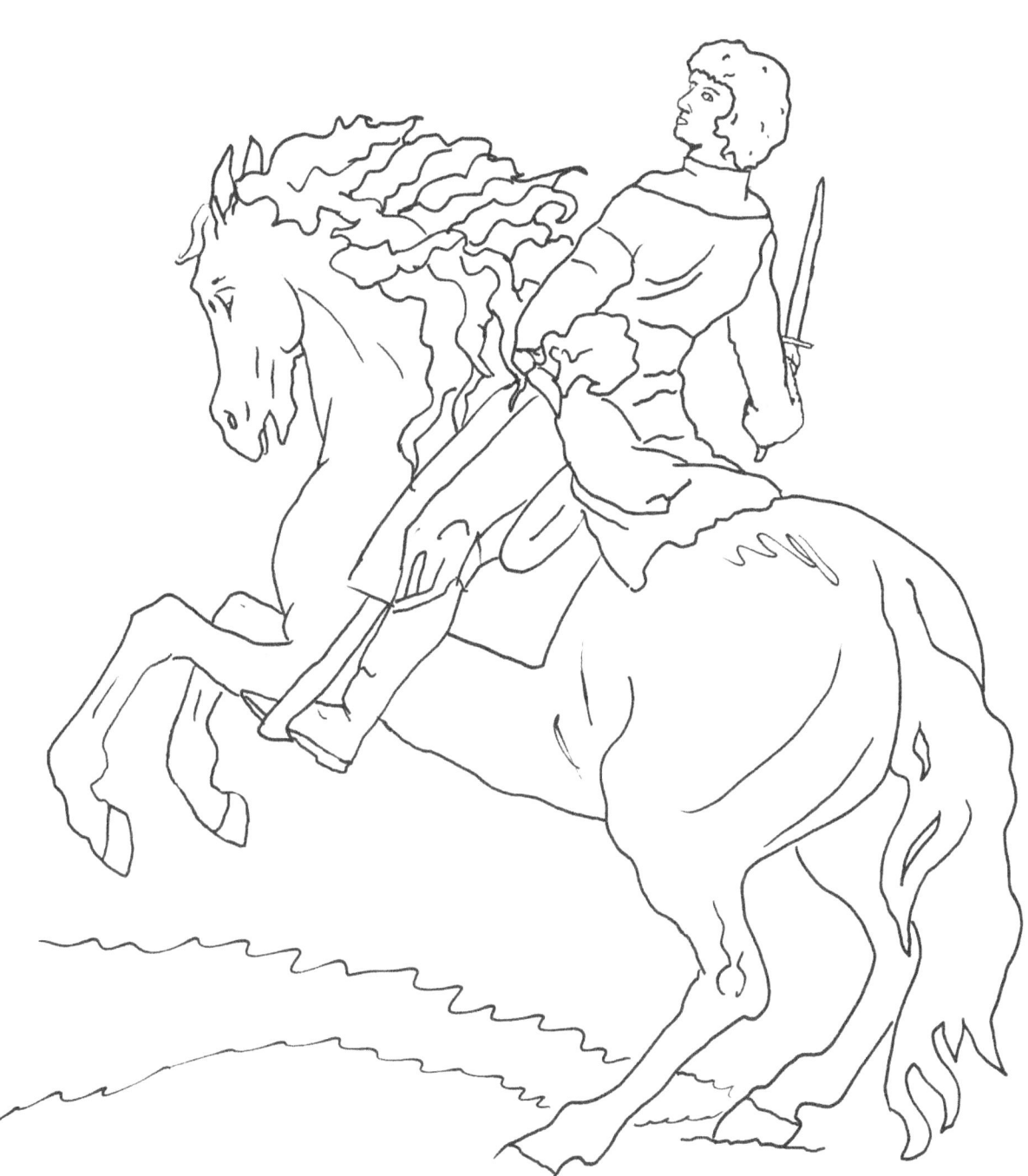

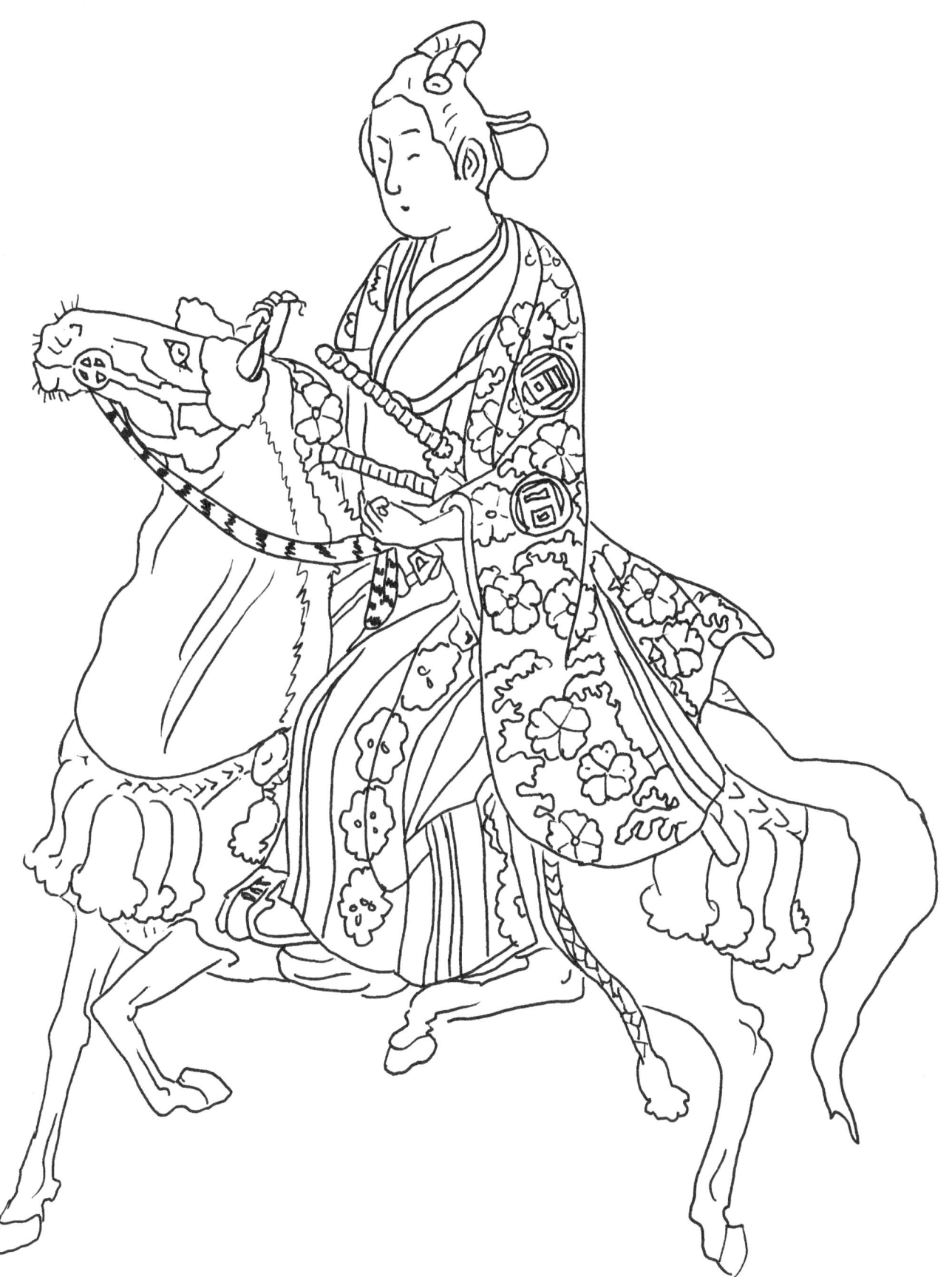

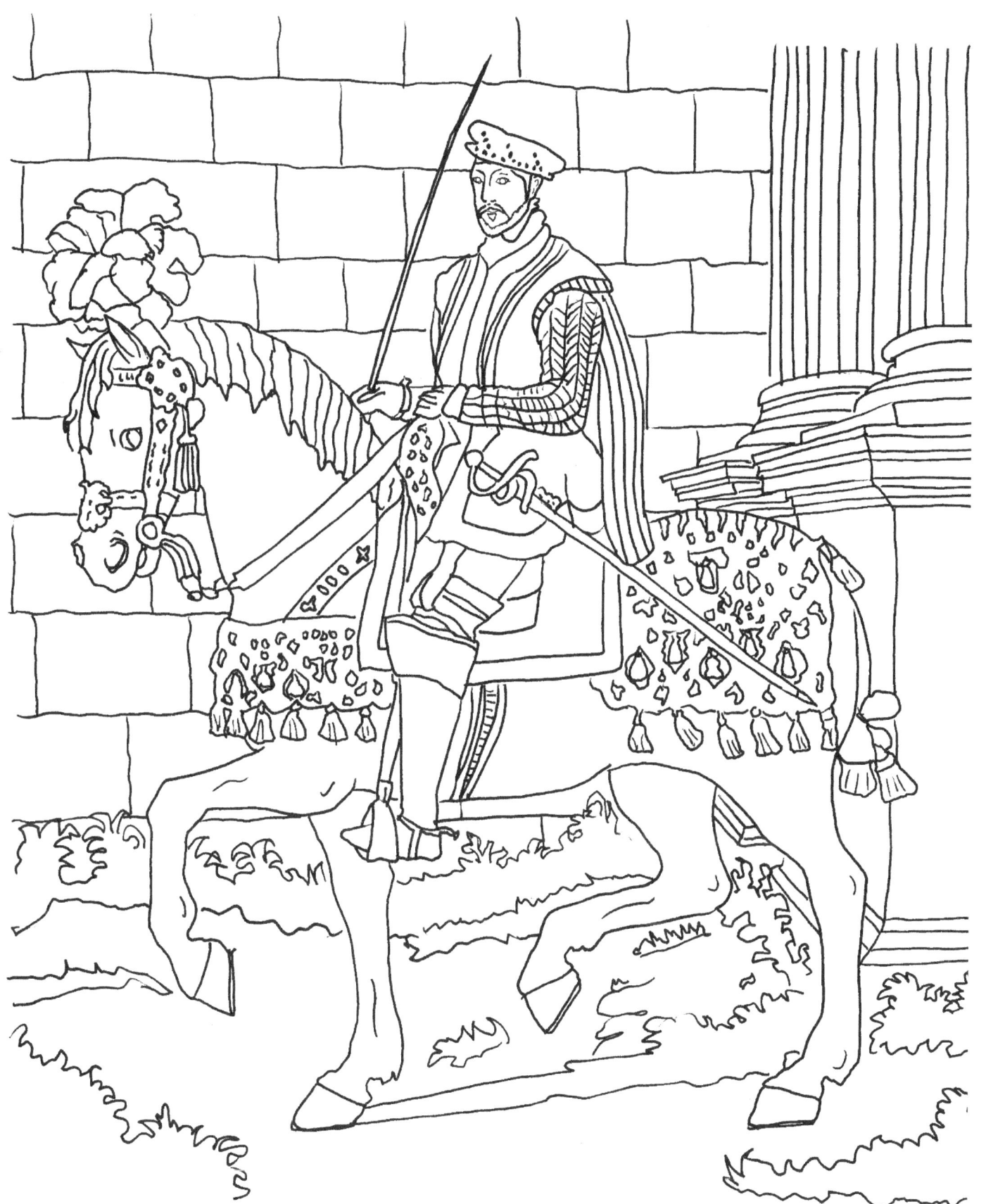

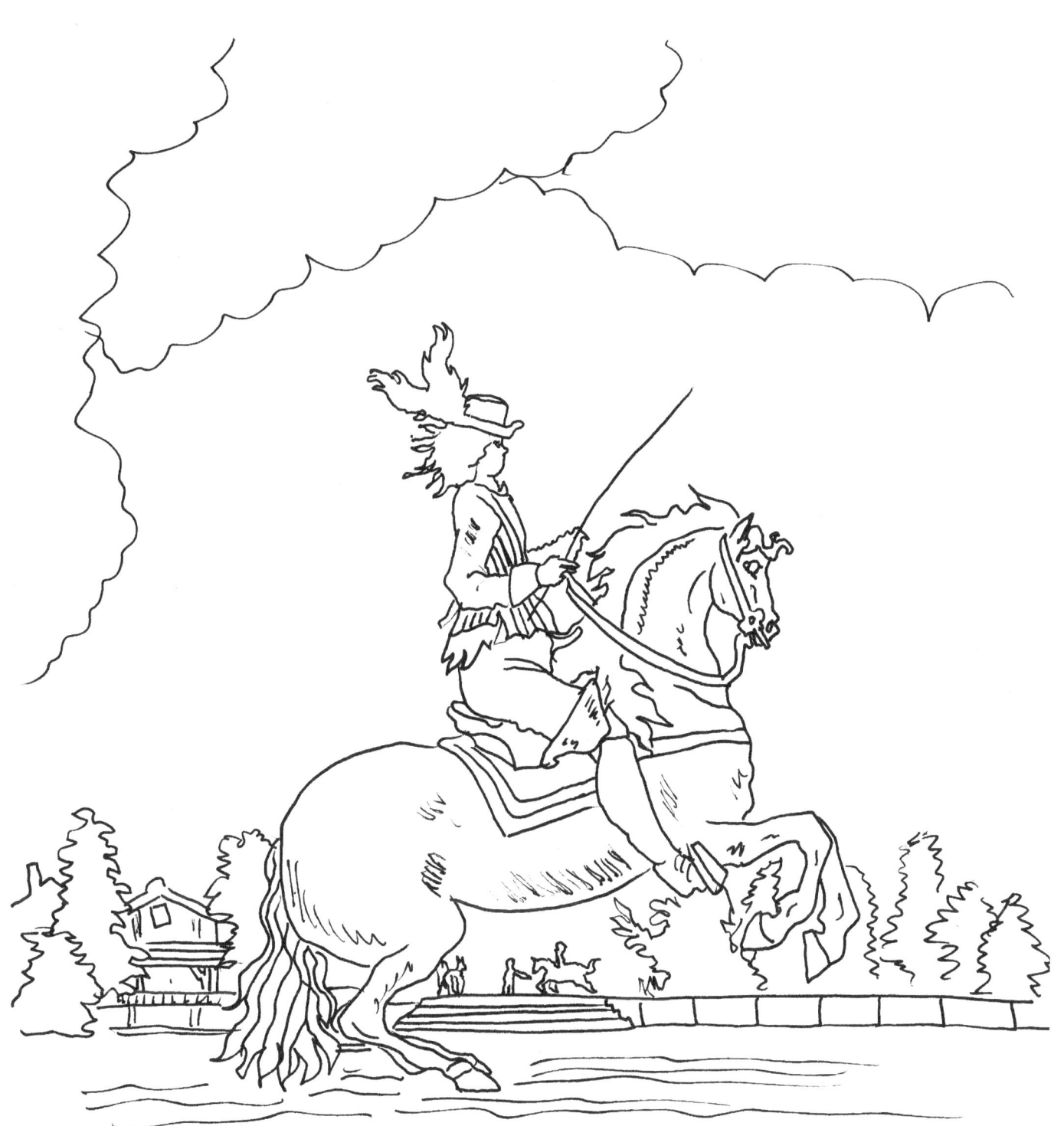

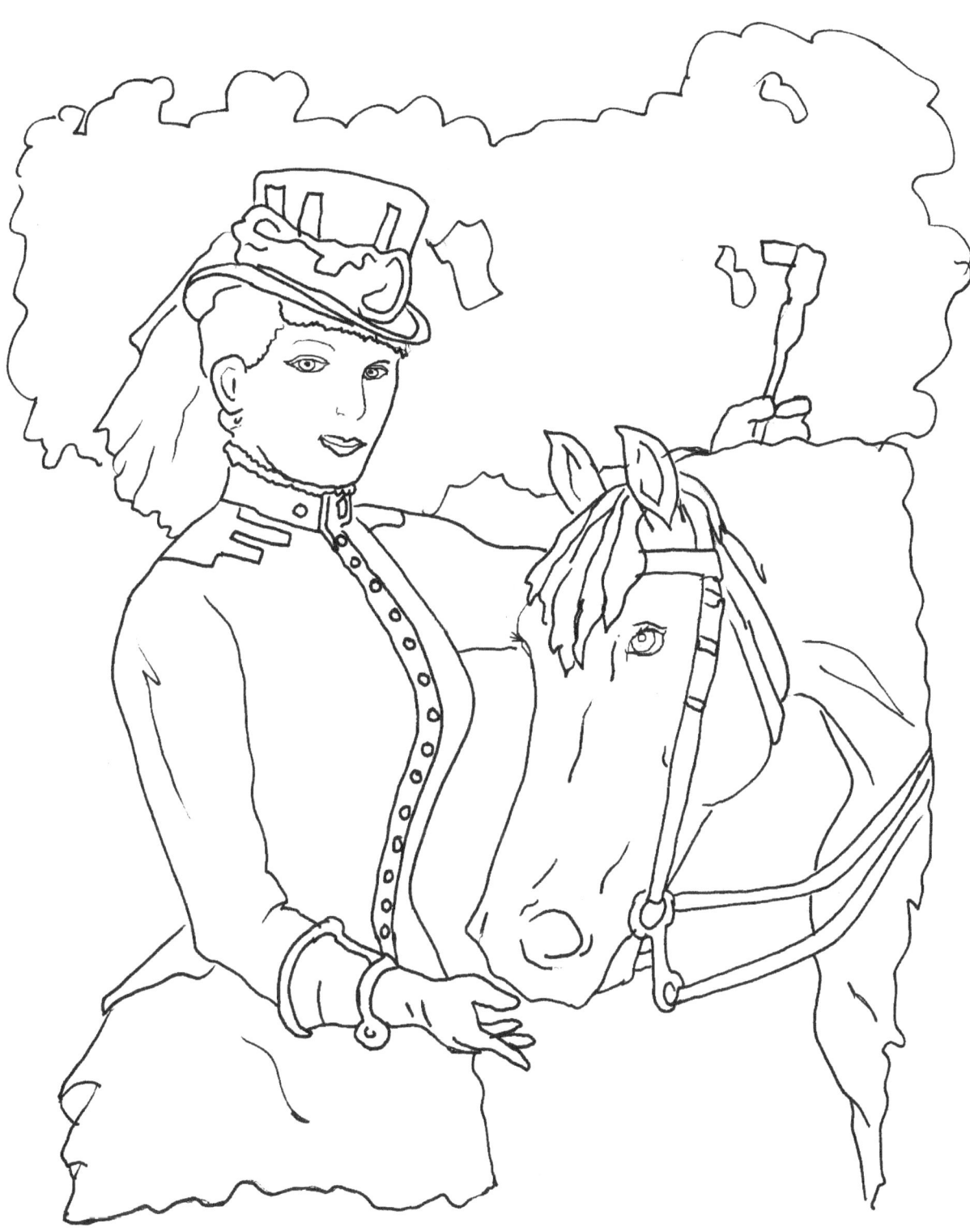

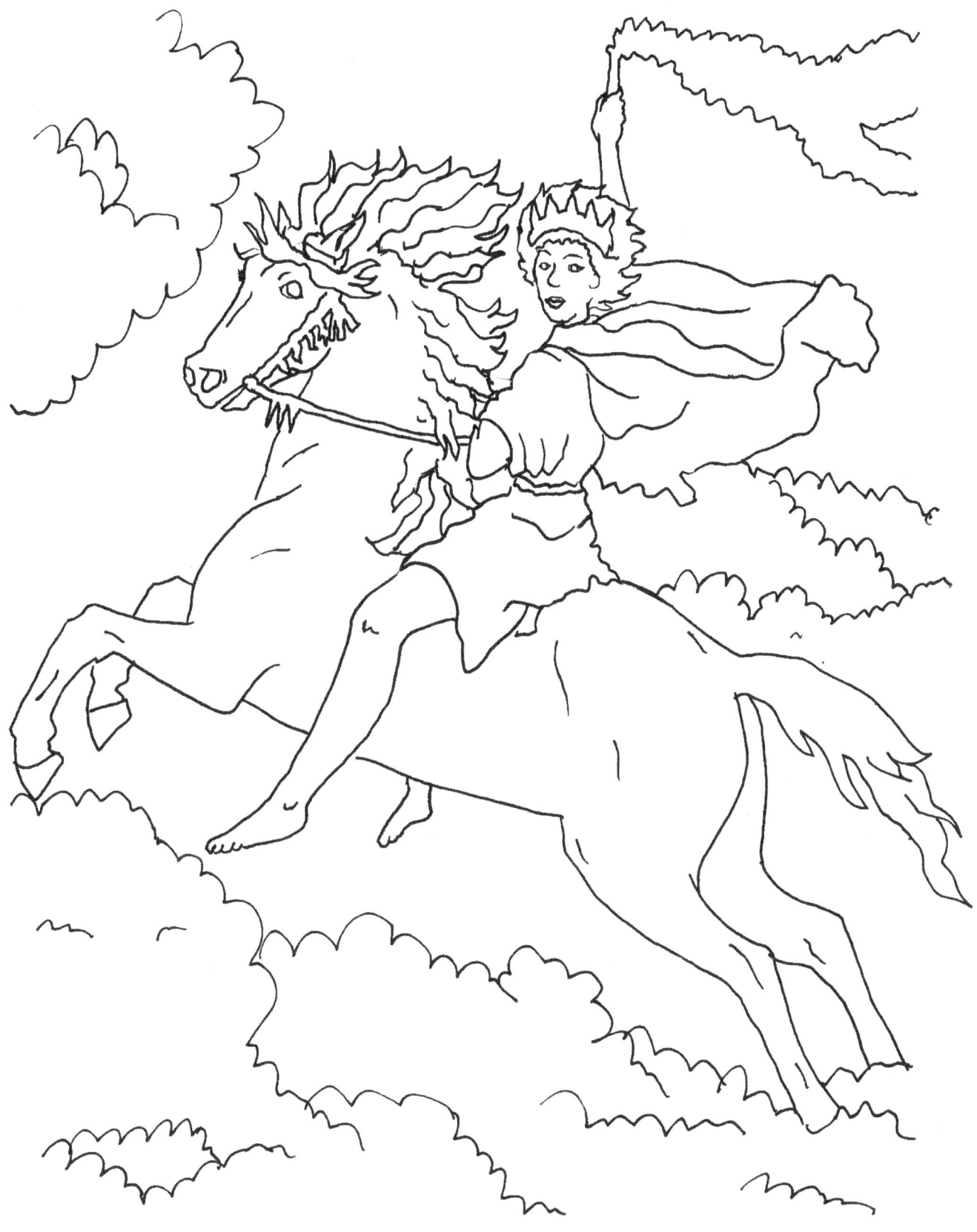

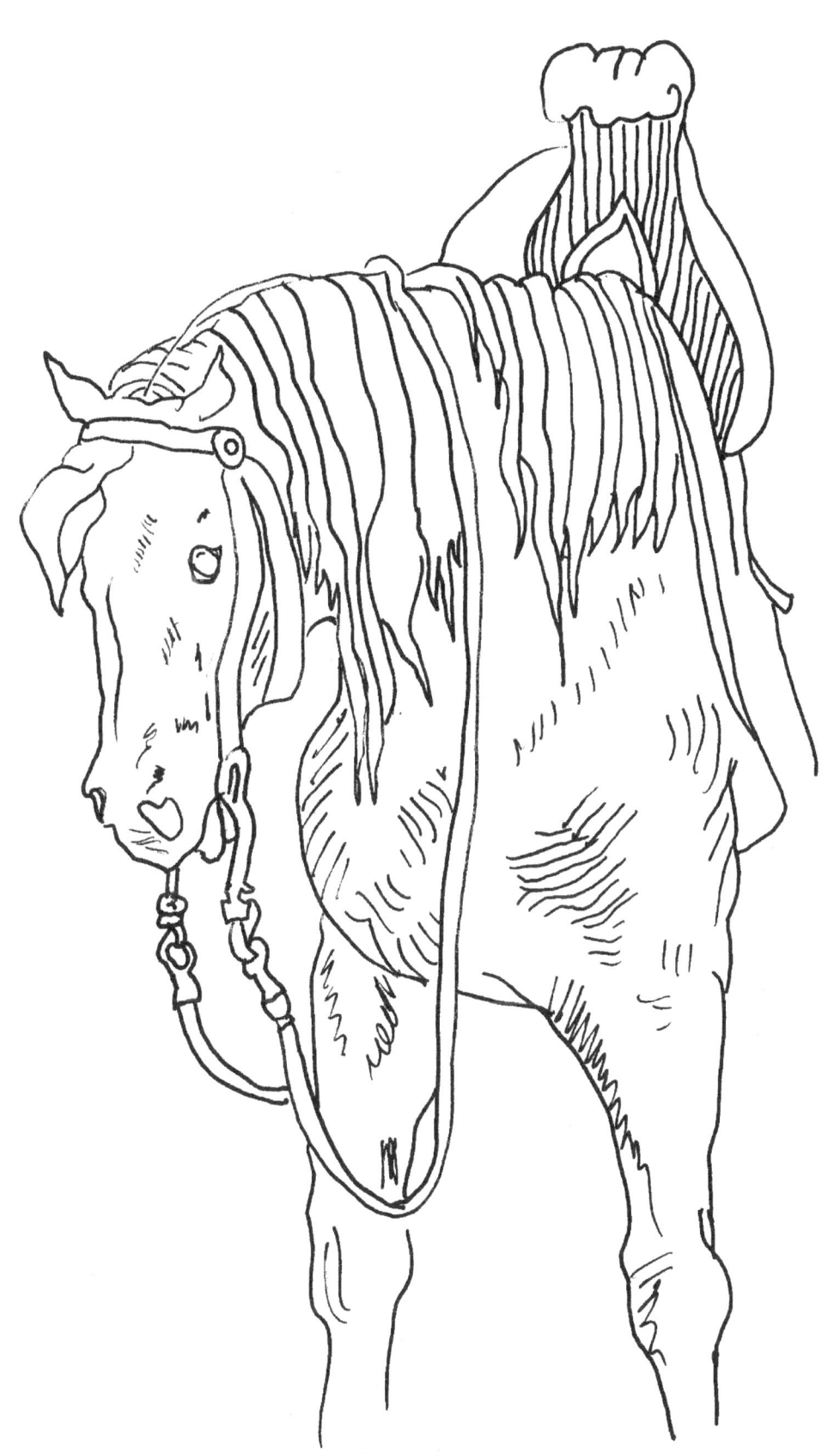

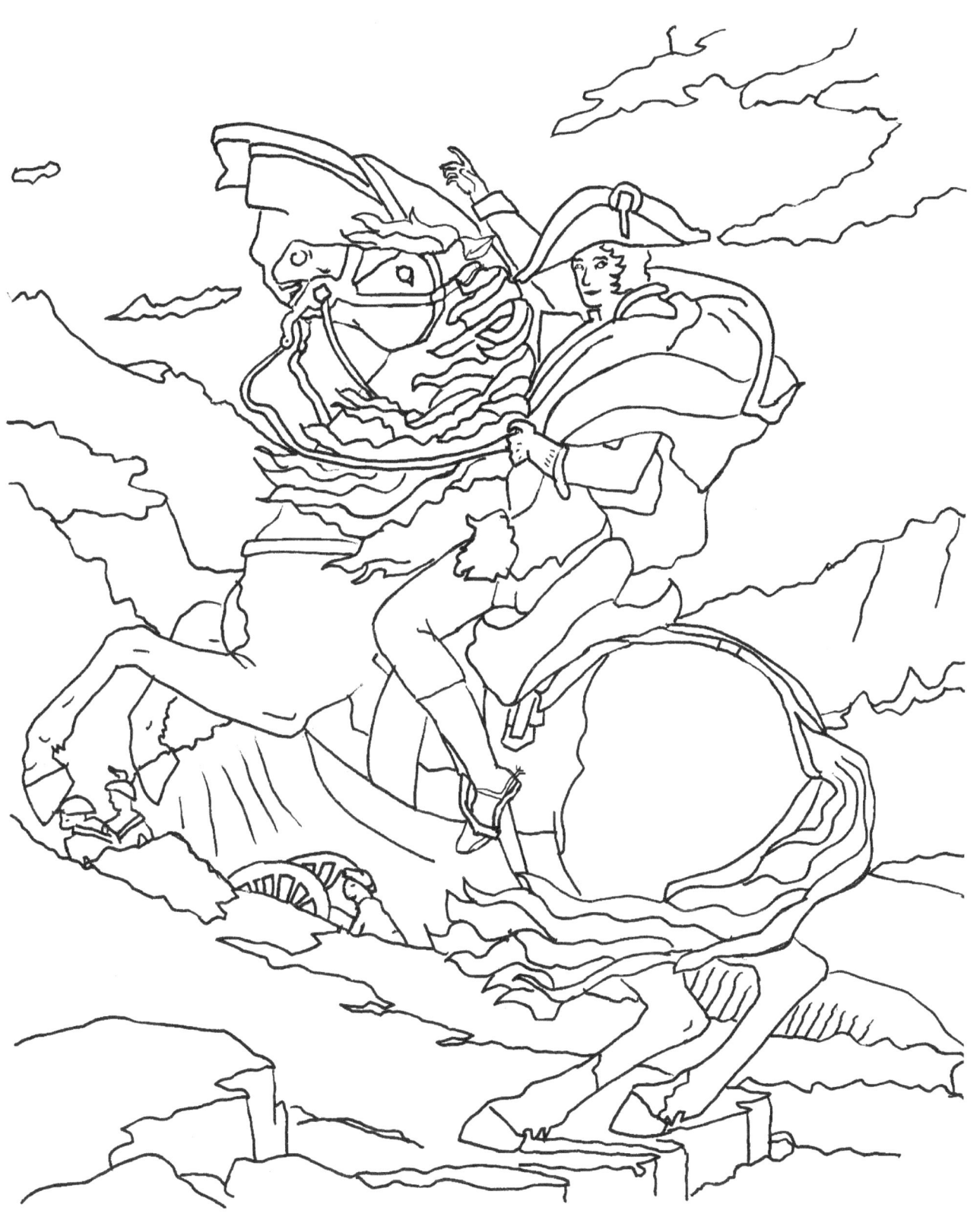

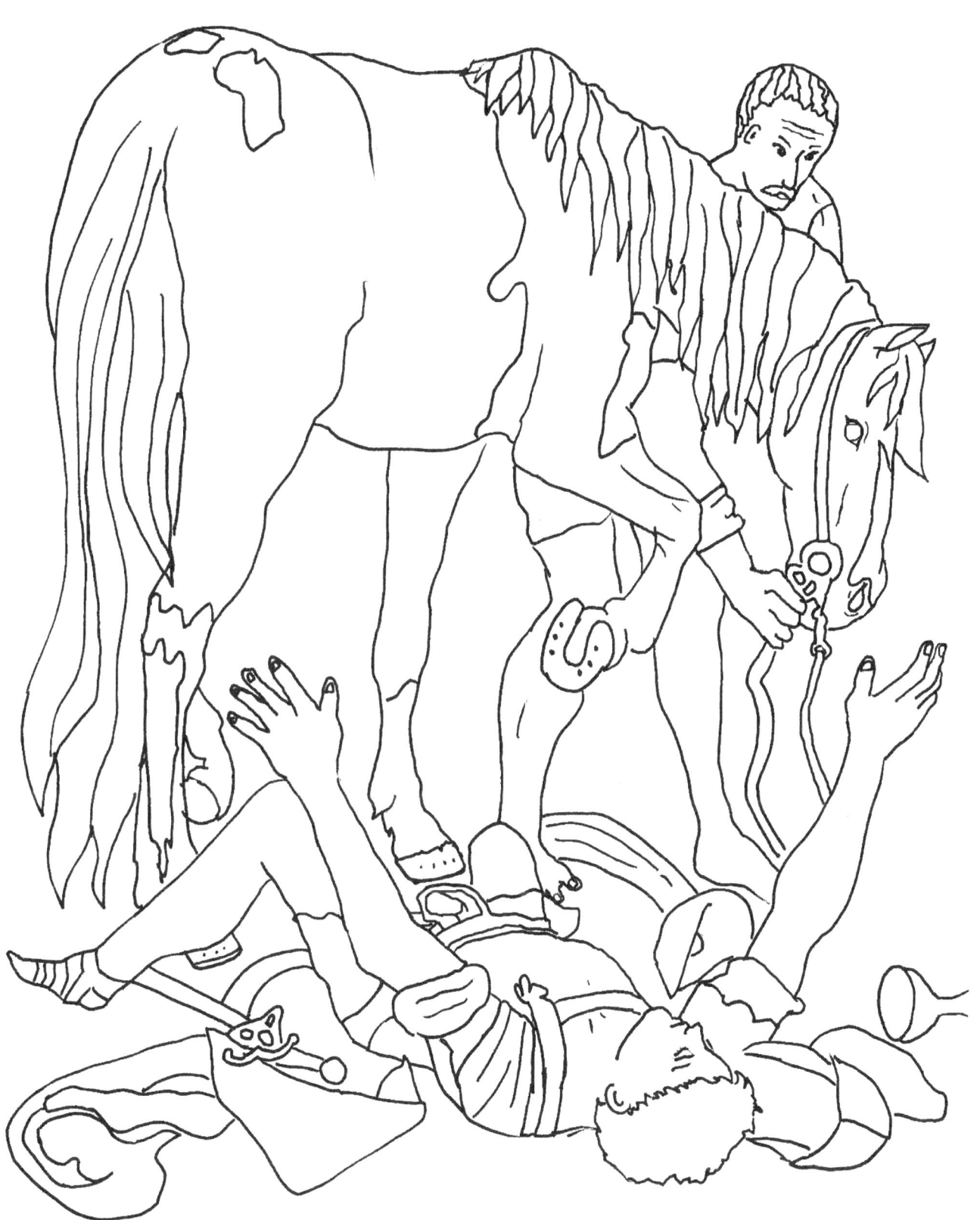

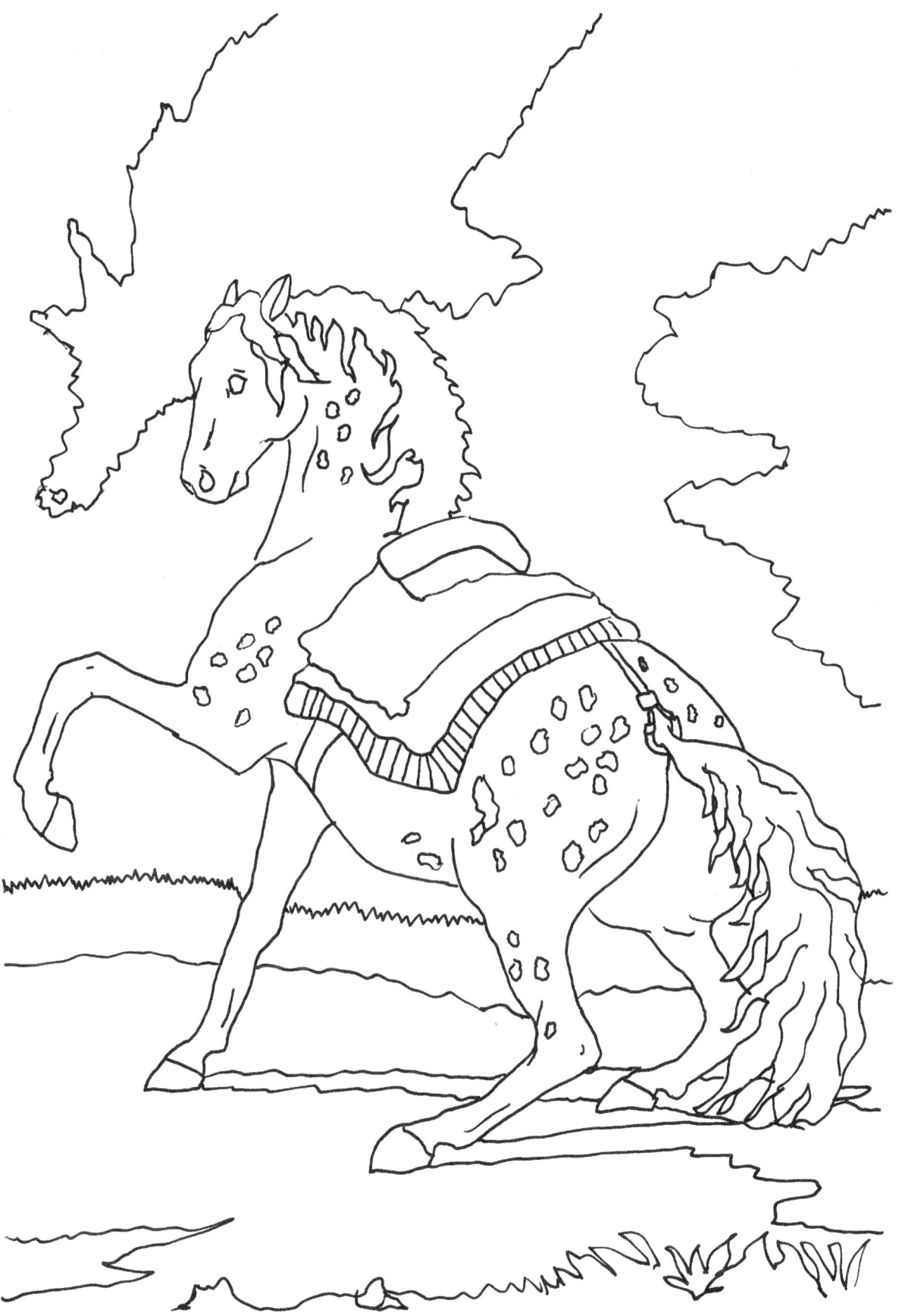

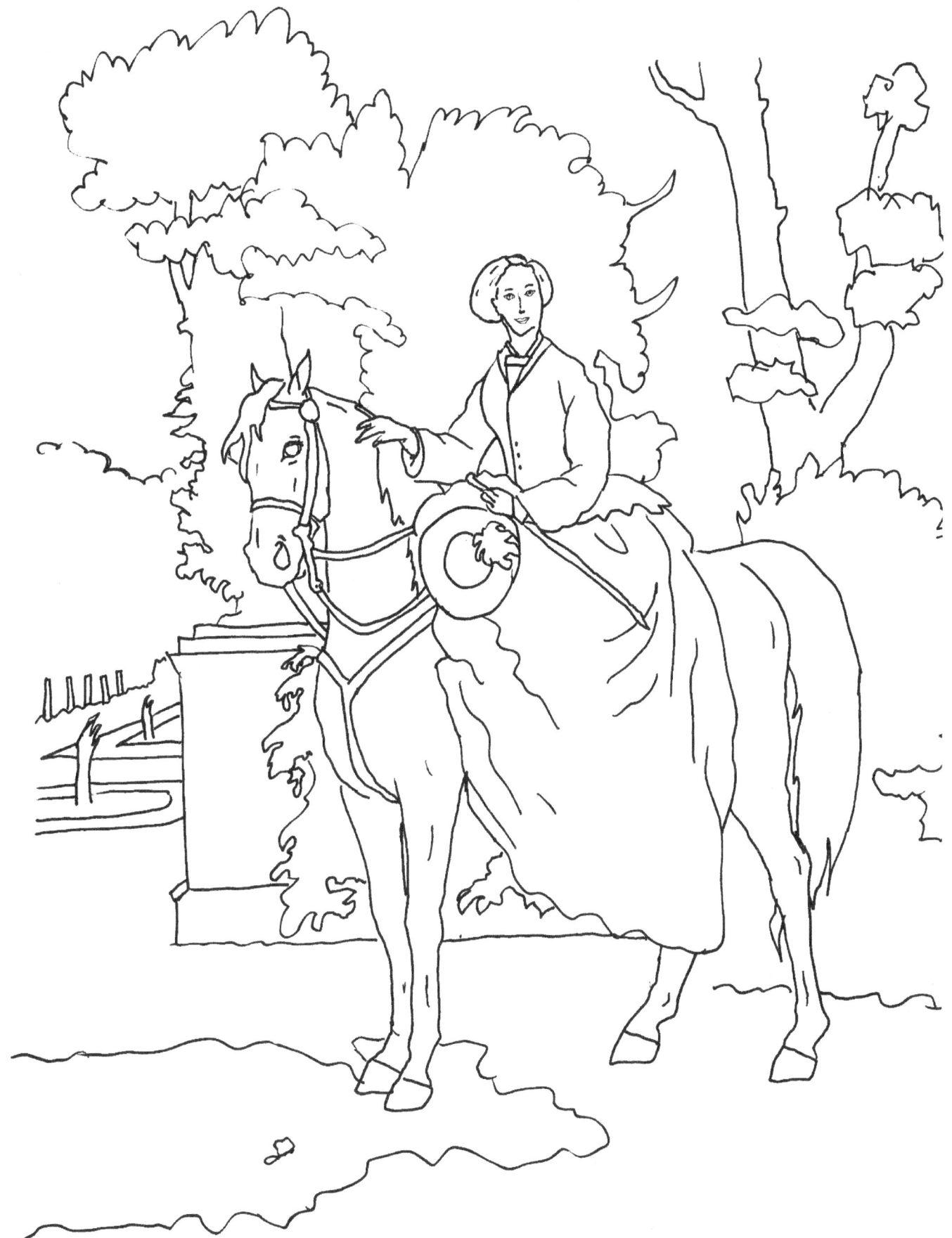

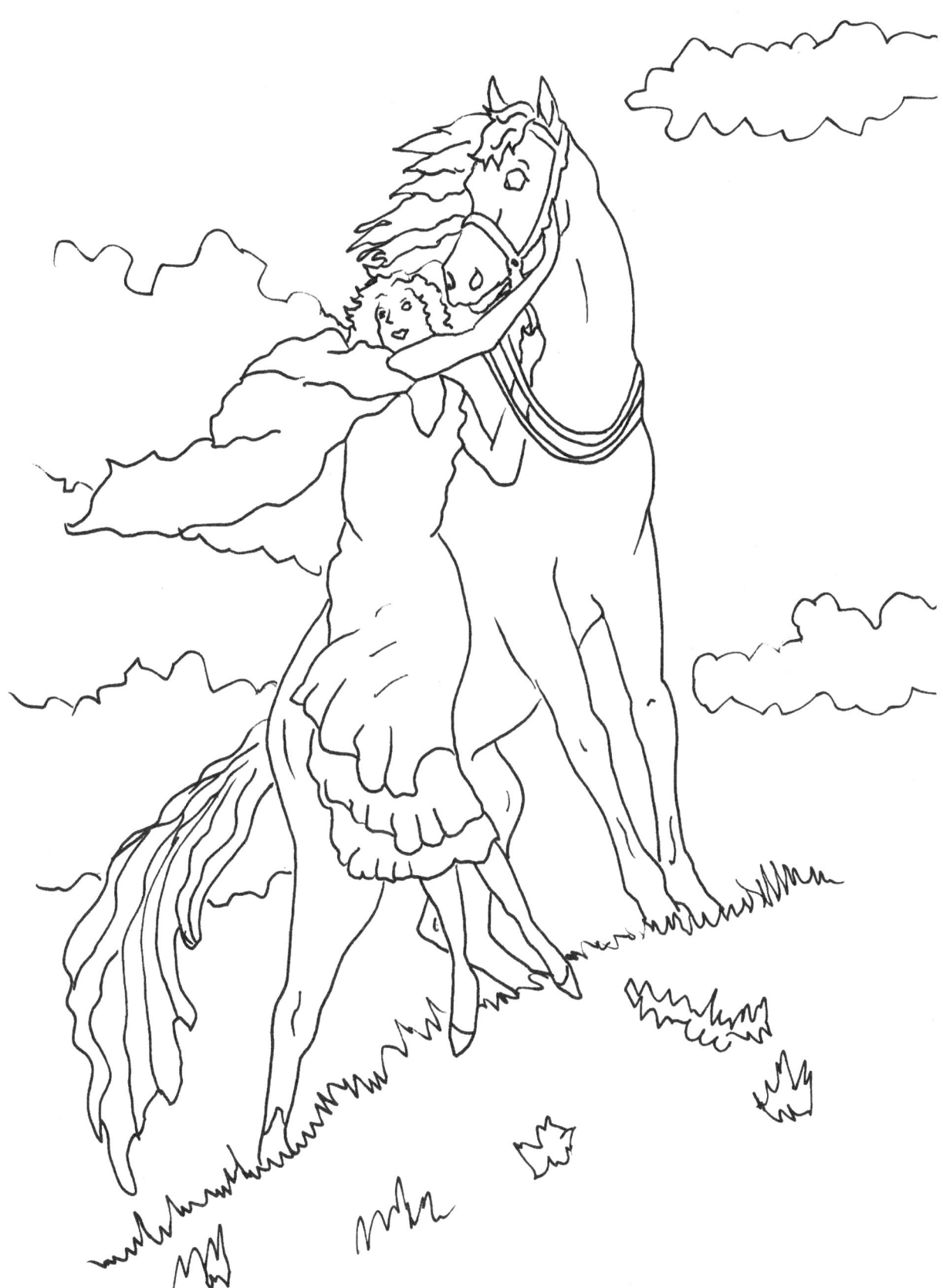

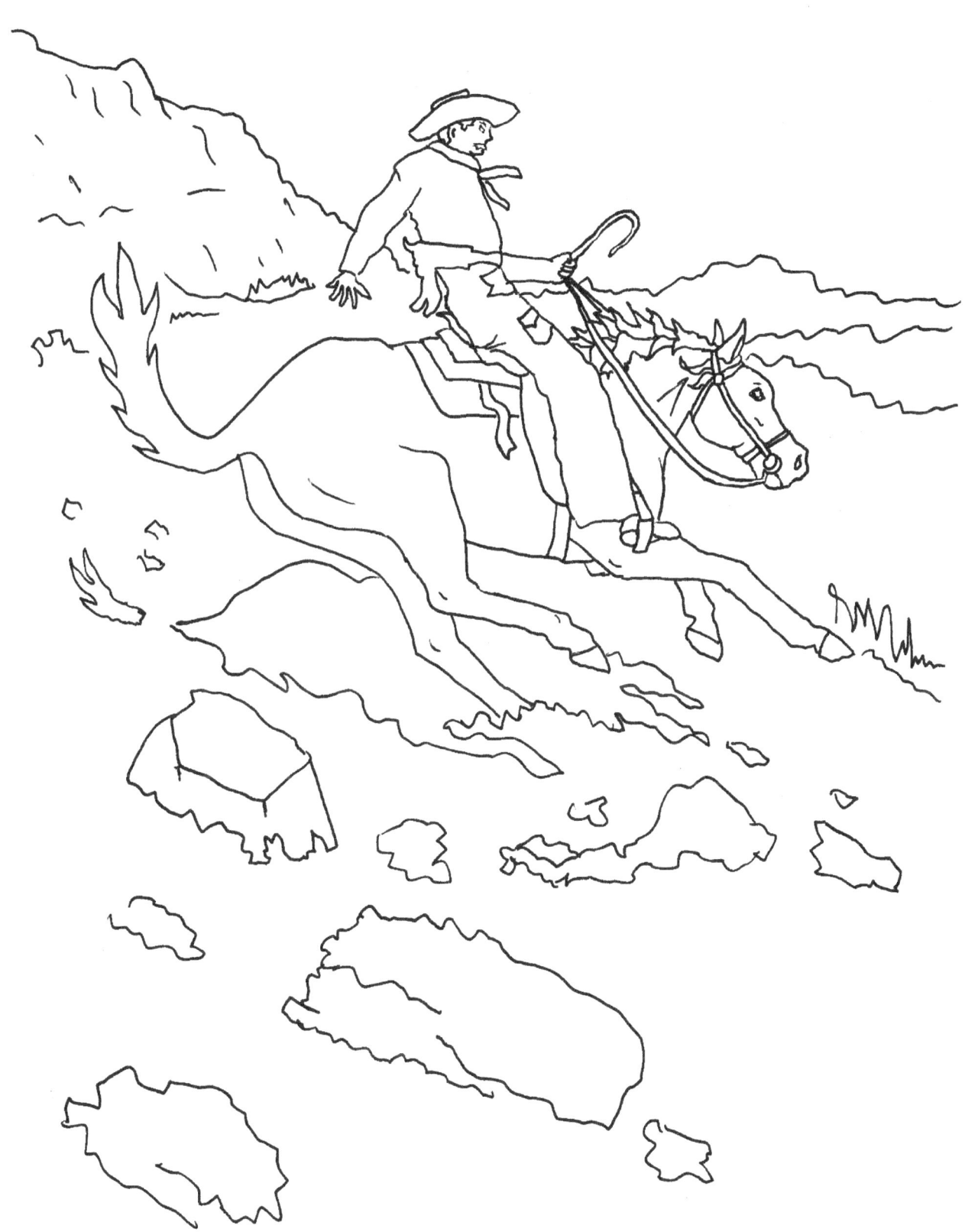

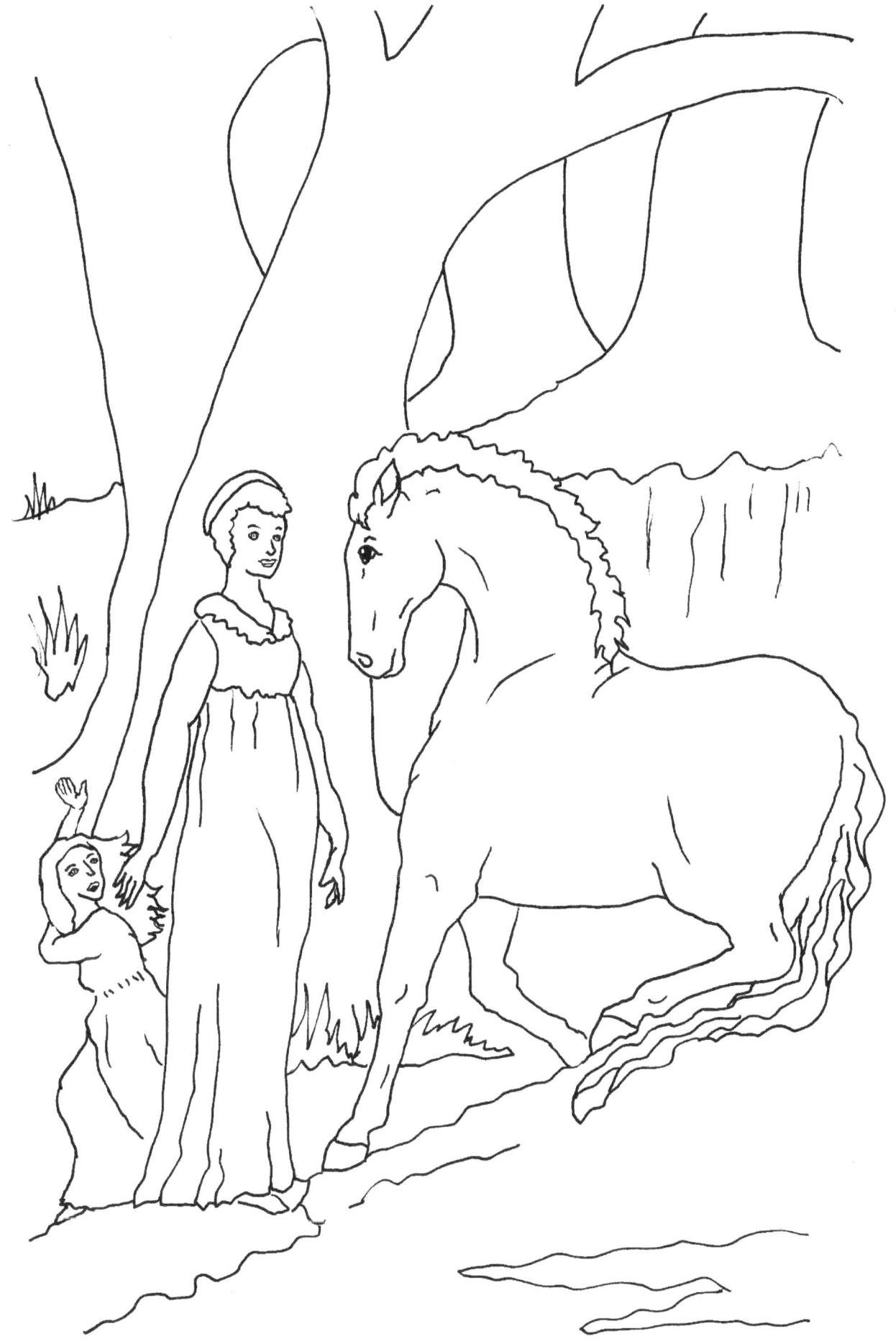

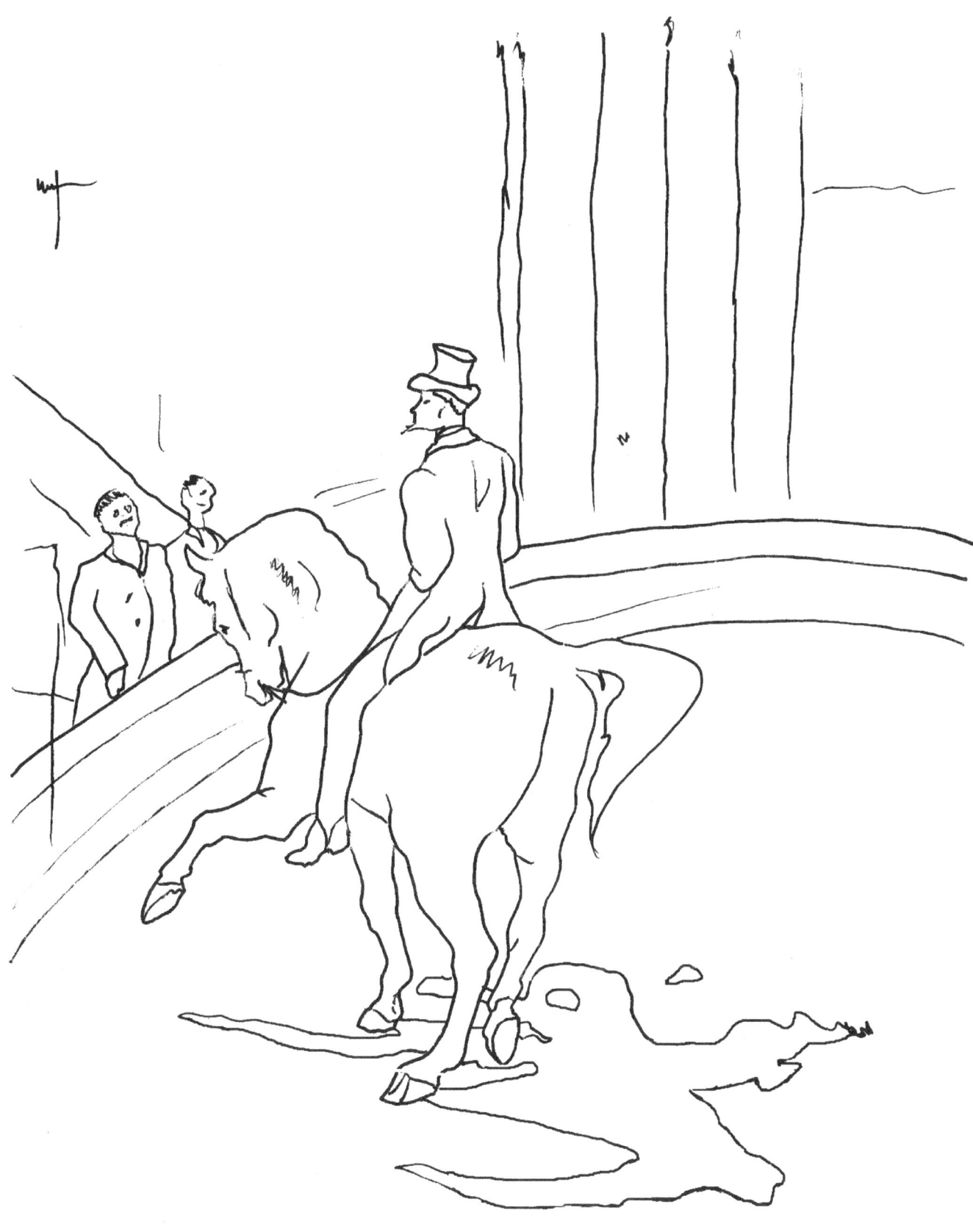

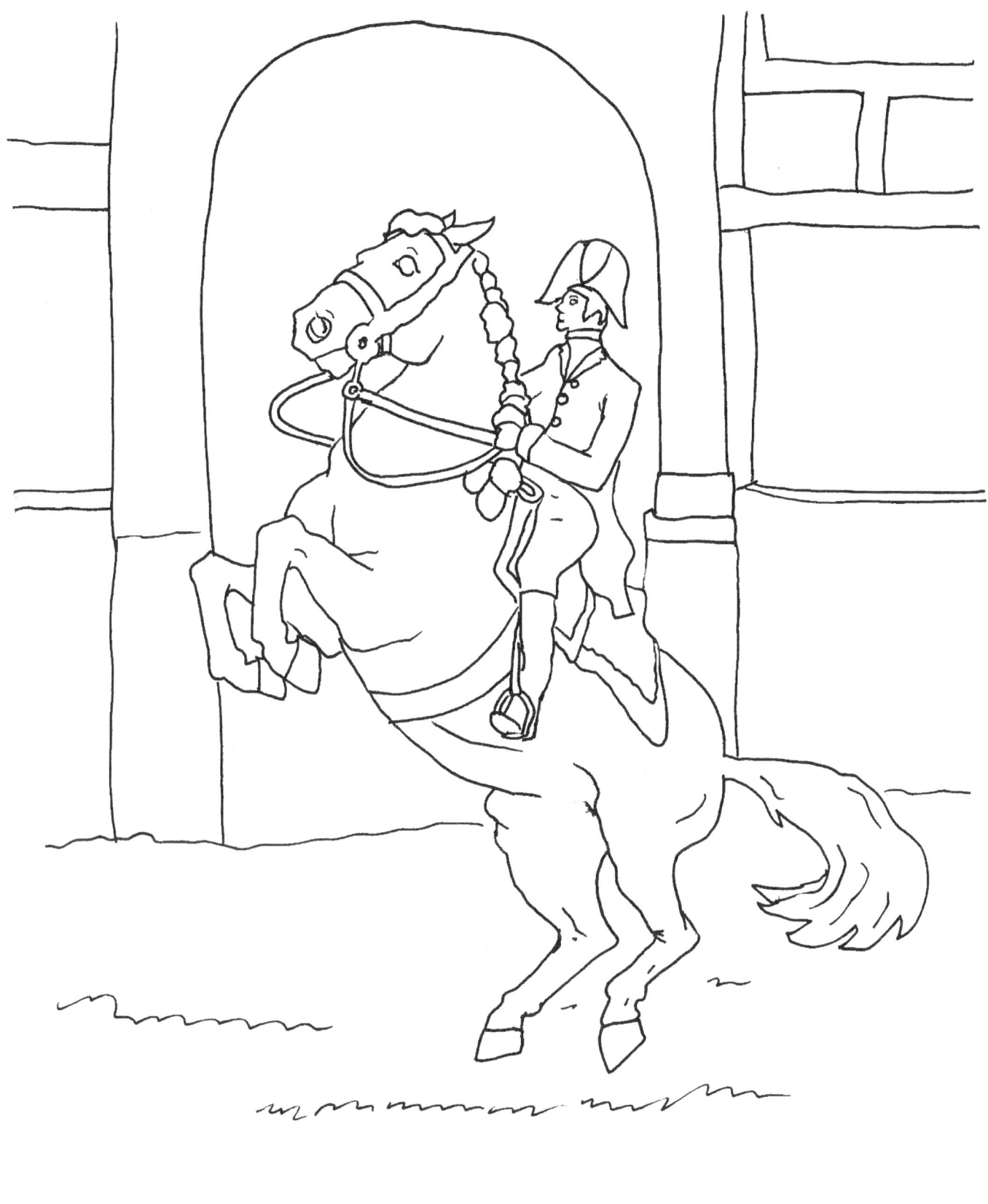

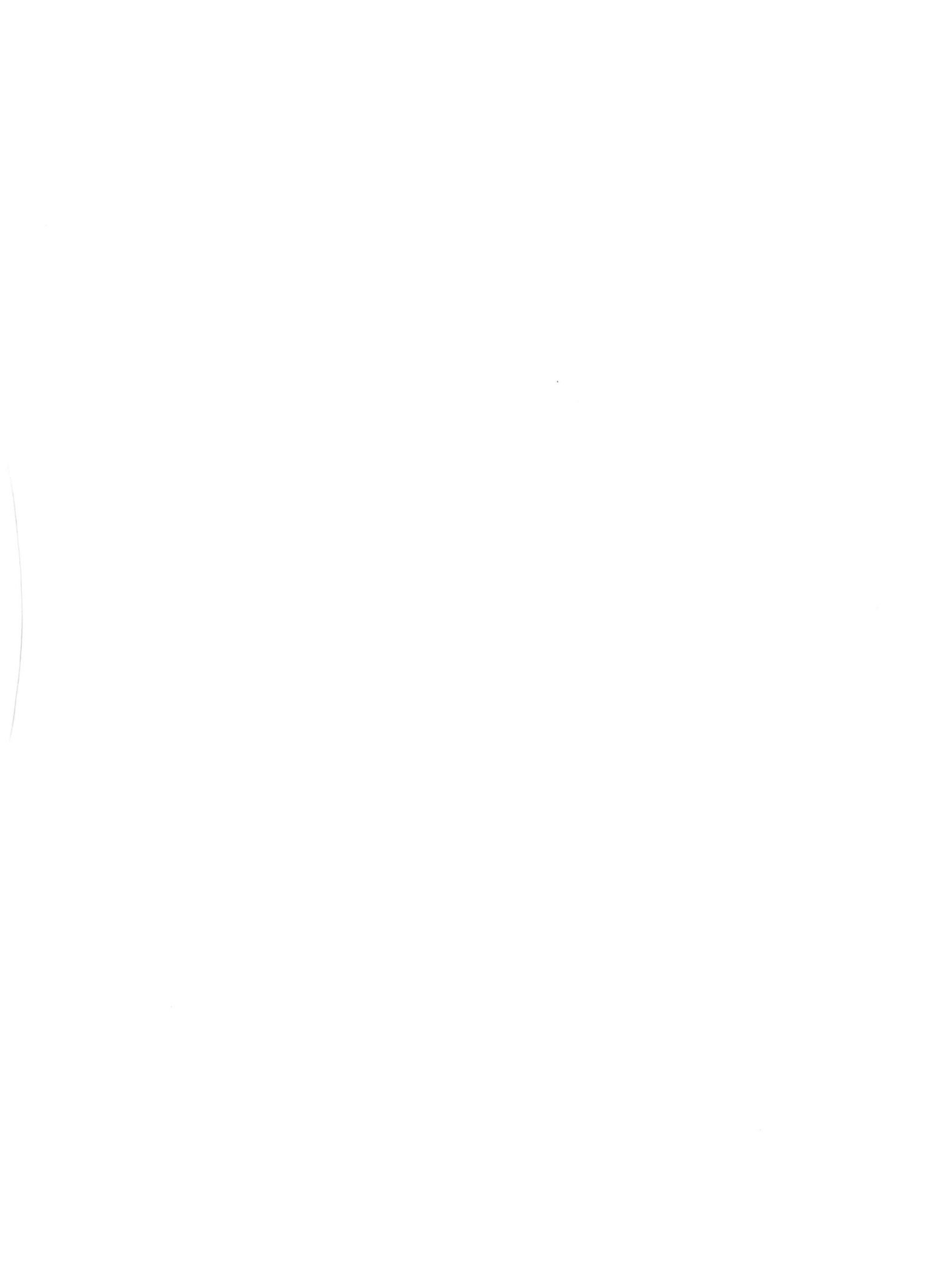